Colors
OF HABITATS

Albatros

Contents

Prelude

Who wouldn't like to explore all the nooks and crannies the world has to offer? And there are quite a lot of them! In some places, it's best to wear only a shirt, while others require you to put on a raincoat or warm fur parka. But has it ever occurred to you that the fact that some places are cold while others are hot, or that some experience heavy rains and others barely see a single raindrop, means that individual regions put on their own colorful coats, too?

Far beyond the polar circle where it's freezing cold,
ice sheets shroud endless plains in pure white.
Meanwhile, oceans are teeming with multi-colored
fish and corals, gently bobbing on the waves. In desert
sand dunes where it's hot and arid due to the golden
sunrays, faded acacia and succulent leaves save
their water for tomorrow, maybe even the day after
tomorrow … On the other hand, wet jungles have
no lack of moisture. Just like meadows, they light
up with a palette of the brightest colors whenever
it rains. To make some sense of all this beauty,
people have named many colors after the habitats they
most resembled: that's how color names like forest
green, savannah beige and even swamp brown saw
the light of the day! Can you find any other shades
such as these?

6

Arctic blue

deep sea blue

glacier blue

snow white

polar bear white

frozen grass

snow petrel

Arctic tern

iceberg

humpback whale

snow goose

blue whale

narwhal

giant squid

orca

muskox

reindeer

bearberry

tufted hairgrass

annual meadow grass

Antarctic pearlwort

cool blue

ink blue

mirage blue

winter breath

polar white

blue whale

snowy owl

snowy albatross

Dall sheep

Arctic ground squirrel

common murre

Polar regions

Arctic poppy

Antarctic fur seal

Scratch, scratch! Frosts scrape the *ice* with their polar hands, maliciously stinging *birds* beneath their black-and-white jackets. Whoo, whoo, the wind blows, the snow-white *bear* roars, and his cry turns into pillars of ice in the sea waves. Today and tomorrow …

chinstrap penguin

polar bear

Arctic hare

emperor penguin

ice floe

walrus

polar fox

elephant seal

leopard seal

8

raccoon grey

glacier grey

cranberry

rusty orange

evergreen

north forest

European larch

mountain goat

great grey owl

wolf

Scots pine

dwarf mountain pine

subalpine fir

Norway spruce

common crane

wild yak

beaver

ferns

moose

zander

lingonberry

common goldeneye

grizzly bear

northern river otter

brown trout

river lamprey

pine green

jade green

wolf grey

beaver brown

pure white

cold water

jade

beryl

nephrite

golden eagle

ibex

taiga bean goose

silver birch

Taiga

Hey, hey! The taiga's calling, roaring with the deep voice of a *bear*, and in the cold, *nephrite* eyes squint, telling stories of forests. On scarred rocks, *ibex* frolic and grey *wolves* howl: A-oo, taiga, the cold beauty of the North—we fall at your feet!

blue spruce

Alpine sedge

Siberian tiger

bog Labrador tea

victory onion

Alpine meadow-grass

Siberian weasel

raccoon

common garter snake

ammonite fossil

chinchilla

pin cushion moss

10

peat brown

mud brown

swamp brown

brown green

heather

stonish beige

alder

hen harrier

mountain pine

nightjar

wood horsetail

bog-rosemary

toad

whinchat

bog asphodel

common crane

peat moss

purple moor-grass

common snipe

gorse

marsh calla

bog iron

goldmoss stonecrop

common club moss

iron ore

brownish orange

dark yellow

reed grass

misty blue

reflecting pond

emperor dragonfly

green hairstreak

marsh fritillary

cup lichen

Peatbog

A *crane* is flying over the wetlands, singing a ballad of still water to *alders, foxgloves* rippling like water, and the *toad*? Ribbet-ribbet, sending its wishes to the bushes. The sun is setting, and the evening land falls asleep in the arms of roaming rivers.

bog cotton

bog wood

raft spider

heather

fringed water lily

white water-crowfoot

foxglove

giant rhubarb

woollyfruit sedge

reed

12

moss green

leaf green

deep brown

forest green

walk in the woods

dark wood

black arches

smoky quartz

acorns

Eurasian hobby

oak tree

Eurasian blue tit

wild boar

marmelade hoverfly

wood forget-me-not

wild garlic

red deer

wood anemone

black woodpecker

lily-of-the-valley

tinder fungus

wood sorrel

red wood ant

summer cep

liverwort

male fern

rowan

blueberry

golden mushroom

bark brown

chestnut brown

brown red

acorn brown

honey brown

red squirrel

honeycomb

hornbeam leaf

beech

Norway maple

Eurasian jay

European green woodpecker

eagle-owl

Deciduous forest

"Scree, scree, winter's coming!" screams a scared *jay*.
Silent, the forest murmurs to the rhythm of brooks
and springs. The *deer* look up, chewing on *sorrel*. "It's said to
be lucky," a *fox* lectures. *Ants* can't hear, stocking their pantry
with *blueberries*. Hush, the forest rustles, sighing in red
rowanberries.

beechnut

red-brown longhorn beetle

herb-paris

honey fungus

horse-chestnut tree leaf

gingko

European hedgehog

common haircap

chestnuts

fly amanita

Roman snail

Devil's bolete

red fox

14

water lily

ash blue

fish pond

water blue

kingfisher blue

mallard green

poplar admiral

lesser purple emperor

black poplar

Canada goose

yellow water-lily

mute swan

kingcup

white willow

white stork

Hydrometra bug

mallard

goat willow

muskrat

northern pike

great diving beetle

sterlet

green frog

fire salamander

duck mussel

yellow perch

common carp

pondweed

willow tree shade

cattail brown

poplar green

willow tree green

frog green

celandine yellow

banded demoiselle

tree swallow

little ringed plover

dwarf lake iris

Lake

great blue heron

Drooping *willow*! What is it you're looking
for at the bottom of the lake? *Perch* gold, mouths
of plump *carps*, yawning *clams*, or just ordinary sand?
Head down, the wise willow stays silent. What would
you know, lippy *irises*, what would you know of living
without shores … of living at the bottom?

hairy spurge

lesser
celandine

smooth
newt

spring snowflake

European
crayfish

great crested grebe

river
kingfisher

bulrush

white water lily

painted turtle

reed

spring fog

cornflower blue

light rose

petal dust

pastel mint

young leaf

fireflies

song thrush

common hazel

western yellow wagtail

seven-spot ladybird

cross spider

swallowtail caterpillar

six-spot burnet

buff-tailed bumblebee

dog rose

clouded Apollo

heath fritillary

Eurasian skylark

ribwort plantain

wild privet

giant peacock moth

common cowslip

spreading bellflower

plumeless thistle

common dandelion

Saint John's wort

ray grass

chicory

moon daisy

flower nectar

daffodil yellow

dandelion yellow

bumblebee yellow

poppy red

pastel brown

orange tip

peacock butterfly

common blue butterfly

swallowtail

small tortoiseshell

Meadow

On the meadow burnt by field *poppies*, big-eyed *butterflies* set the hearts of *moon daisies* on fire, *chicories* can't forget *briers*, an azure song on their lips. It's summer, the time of *bush crickets*, *wagtails*, *bees*, and *fireflies*. *Ladybugs*, the fortune tellers, fold their fate out of sun locks: Whirly, are we, bird?

speckled wood

Jersey tiger

peppermint

red clover

cock's-foot

daffodil

western honey bee

red poppy

brown hare

great green bush-cricket

nettle

silver thistle

cornflower

meadow cat's tail

common mole

almond white

olive green

olive brown

lavender

grape

oleander

almond

cork oak

lemon tree

juniper

black-headed gull

sea salt

sea oats

bay tree

common cockles

greater flamingo

Dalmatian pelican

common bottlenose dolphin

harbour crab

barnacle

common squid

sardines

red comb star

blue mussels

hermit crab

manta ray

shortfin mako shark

green sea turtle

citrus orange

lemon yellow

eucalyptus green

dolphin grey

sand yellow

blue lagoon

olives

cypress

oleander

lavender

olive tree

grape vine

The Mediterranean

Fragrant *oranges* put their ears to the lips of *olives*.
The hot day beneath the sun's hands, lying on beaches
on the shore, wondering about the purple magic of *lavenders*.
Chrrrick! *Crickets* and *cicadas* chipper to see who's the best.
Who's to tell?

orange tree

oregano

rosemary

cedar

cicada

fig tree

two-spotted cricket

wormwood

Mediterranean house gecko

wild goat

eucalyptus

sage

oyster shell

turtle green

blue kelp

timid sea

Carribean blue

ocean

limestone rock

needlefish

yellow-lipped
sea krait

seagrass

spotted
manta ray

mermaid's
hair algae

krill

common clownfish

sea anemone

leafy
seadragon

coralline
algae

organ
pipe coral

longnose
butterflyfish

bay scallop

yellowmouth moray

soft tree coral

fire coral

blue coral

staghorn coral

chalice coral

long-snouted seahorse

Achilles tang

spiny starfish

brain coral

sea pen

giant clam

nautilus

bright purple

navy blue

coral red

neon orange

starfish

bright yellow

tiger

shark

blue-green chromis

jellyfish

sea whip coral

convict tang

moorish idol

jewel damselfish

Hawaiian cleaner wrasse

Coral reefs

Shhh, shhh, the eternal heart of oceans murmurs,
gentle *jellyfishes* dancing gracefully, up and down;
Careful, *lionfish*! Don't mess up their figures!
Deep down, at the dark sandy bottom, lonely *shells*
and *turtles*. Shhh, shhh, the ocean
consoles them in their grief …

Caulerpa seaweed

red lionfish

long-spine porcupinefish

bubble coral

hawksbill sea turtle

red asparagus algae

oyster

tube coral

octopus

sheet coral

sea cucumber

cauliflower coral

sheer sunlight

termite beige

Sahara sand

pale leaf

palm tree

pear cactus

demantoid

gold

sand dune

tamarisk

camel thorn tree

sand cat

desert hyacinth

Bactrian camel

spinifex grass

nine-banded armadillo

field bindweed

Kalahari melon

fennec fox

meerkats

red kangaroo

Indian porcupine

tumbleweed

termite mound

Hoodia succulent

termite

bronze

warm sand

sand brown

desert grey

dull brown

dusty grey

baobab

burrowing owl

white-backed vulture

dates

Desert

The sun presses its hot face into the golden *sand*,
breathing, in and out, in the stuffy air. Atop *baobabs*,
a *vulture* looks out for the faraway rain,
counting down the days … And in the warm breeze,
tumbleweeds roll, spreading their tumbles
in all scorching directions.

addax

date palm

dromedary

saguaro cactus

prickly pear

central bearded dragon

barrel cactus

desert tortoise

papyrus

black desert cobra

Echeveria succulent

Mongolian gerbil

greater Egyptian jerboa

desert lily

deathstalker scorpion

Sacred scarab

flower of stone

savannah beige

savannah green

acacia green

khaki

crocodile green

shrub green

gum acacia

Thomson's gazelle

cheetah

Raggiana bird-of-paradise

vervet monkey

caracal

elephant

Triodia

plains zebra

spotted hyena

giraffe

black cobra

ostrich

lion

black rhinoceros

raw zircon

elephant grey

ostrich feather

lion's den

gazelle brown

gold

sunset gold

lilac-breasted roller

rubber vine

Gouldian finch

European bee-eater

calliandra

fish eagle

Savannah

Hisss, a snake crawls in the tall grass, the *cobra* queen right next to the *lion* king. Roar! His mighty cry rips through the savannah, and scared *birds* disappear in the clouds, while a small *vervet monkey*, safe in its *acacia*, spitefully laughs at everyone and everything.

giraffe

giant rat's tail grass

hippopotamus

grey crowned crane

bat-eared fox

white sage

African sacred ibis

water buffalo

Nile crocodile

lion's tail

beardgrass

jungle green

fiery orange

warm black

vivid yellow

avocado green

green banana

jaguar

Cattleya orchid

scarlet macaw

bird of paradise

bamboo

resplendent quetzal

coffee tree

harlequin poison frog

Queen Victoria's water lily

turquoise

pineapple

black caiman

bromelia

calla lily

corpse plant

green iguana

green anaconda

Goliath bird-eating spider

blue poison dart frog

quetzal green

poison green

sapphire blue

turquoise

hot pink

scarlet red

sparkling violetear

hyacinth macaw

pale-throated sloth

coconut tree

spider monkey

Nepenthes

strangler fig

Menelaus blue morpho

monarch butterfly

Rainforest

A geyser of colors is swirling in the jungle, rampaging. *Parrots* show off their fiery feathers, *toucans* hit *coconuts*. Have fun with us on endless *lianas*! In the tropical shadow, have a sip of *pineapple* juice. Hurray, the jungle feast is just about to start!

guava

banana plant

toco toucan

black panther

Rafflesia

red-eyed treefrog

Monstera

avocado

heliconia flower

passion flower

Venus flytrap

bat grey

stalagmite

grey moth

limestone white

grim white

toad green

olivine

tissue moth

soda straws

lesser cave spider

ebony spleenwort

American black bear

spotted-tail salamander

greater horseshoe bat

springtails

water horsetail

Pilea nettle

brown long-eared bat

aragonite

striped skunk

Trogloraptor

bird's nest fern

fluorite

selenite

common noctule

red-bellied black snake

hematite

tridymite

cave centipede

common woodlouse

graphite

chalcedony

phosphorus green

glow worm

rose quartz

brownish pink

wind cave

dark grey

stalactite

glow-worm

cave swallow

herald moth

luminous fungi

limestone column

Cave

In a deep cave, *bats* dream their batty dreams, among *dripstones*, dripped into being by long centuries. "Hey, blind *olm*, what can you see?" the merry echo calls out. A *pearl mussel* giving birth to its rare children in the heavy air, for the princess, awaited by a water dragon in the blue lake. Patiently, year after year, quietly, at the bottom of the damp cave …

tiger salamander

Devils Hole pupfish

jasper

pyrite

azurite

spectacle case pearly mussel

stalagmite

olm

marbled salamander larvae

banded sculpin

quartz

rose quartz

Fowler's toad

marbled salamander

Color harmony

Learn how to match colors in harmonic combinations, just like nature itself can. The color wheel will help you. It's a useful tool that allows you to easily find out which colors match and which don't. When colors match, the result is pleasing to the eye. This is called *color harmony*. Color harmony can be achieved with as few as three primary colors: blue, yellow, and red.

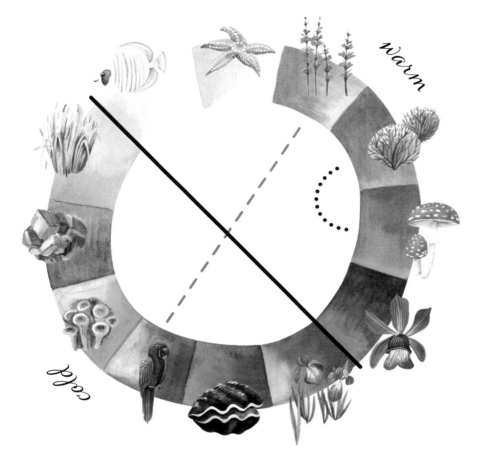

When you select a color and draw a line to the one opposite, they'll match beautifully. That's why such colors are called complementary.

Warm shades (all the way from yellow to red-purple) or cool ones (from purple to yellow-green) also match well.

You can also combine the colors that are placed close to one another.

The inconspicuous shades of brown, cream, white, grey, and slate are more subdued and earthy. Their tones can be easily combined with all other colors.

Take a look at how easily nature matches colors. Try making these or similar color combinations that match beautifully, and create many more, relying only on your own imagination!

colors of autumn leaves

colors of wild fruits

colors of the grass

colors of ice

colors of the sea

colors of the sun

colors of pebbles

colors of sand

© Designed by B4U Publishing for Albatros,
an imprint of Albatros Media Group, 2021.
Na Pankráci 30, Prague 4, Czech Republic
Authors: Jana Sedláčková, Štěpánka Sekaninová
Illustrator: Magdalena Konečná
Printed in Czech Republic by Tiskárna Helbich, a.s.
ISBN 978-80-00-05934-1